Aardvarks

Victoria Blakemore

For Mrs. Jamro, for inspiring a love of reading in my students with story time.

Copyright info/picture credits

Table of Contents

What Are Aardvarks?

Aardvarks are mammals. They are sometimes mistaken for anteaters, but the two animals are not related.

The word aardvark comes from the Afrikaans words for earth and pig. They are sometimes called ant bear, earth pig, or ground pig.

Aardvarks are usually gray and

beige in color.

Size

Aardvarks can be up to seven feet long. Their tail is very long. It is usually between two and three feet in length. They are about two feet tall.

Adults often weigh between 130 and 180 pounds.

Male and female aardvarks

are often about the same

size.

Physical Characteristics

Aardvarks are known for their long **snout**. At the end of their snout, they have special nostrils that they can close when they are digging.

Their large ears allow aardvarks to hear from far away. They can hear and smell insects through the dirt.

Aardvarks have long, strong claws. They are used to dig holes and defend themselves from **predators.**

Habitat

Aardvarks are usually found in grasslands, savannas and woodlands. They need places with lots of insects to eat and dirt to dig their burrows.

They also need somewhere it is not too cold. They have very little fur to protect them from cold temperatures.

Range

Aardvarks are only found on the continent of Africa. They live south of the Sahara desert.

They are often seen in countries like South Africa, Botswana, Nigeria, and Zambia.

Diet

Aardvarks are **insectivores**.

They eat only insects.

Their diet is made up of mainly ants and termites. They have also been known to eat beetles and insect **larvae**. They are thought to prefer termites to other insects.

Aardvarks can eat large quantities of insects. They have been known to eat up to 50,000 termites in a single night.

Aardvarks use their claws to dig into termite mounds. Once they have a hole big enough to stick their snout it, they can eat.

They use their long, sticky tongue to catch the insects. It can be almost twelve inches long.

Large termite mounds can be

home to thousands of termites.

Communication

Aardvarks are usually very quiet animals. They sometimes make grunting sounds. They have also been known to bleat if they are in danger.

Aardvarks have special scent glands. They may use the scent to help them find other aardvarks.

Aardvarks are not often seen communicating with other aardvarks.

Movement

Aardvarks are very good at digging. They can dig long tunnels very quickly. It takes them only ten minutes to dig a hole and completely cover themselves.

Aardvarks can walk several miles each night looking for food.

Aardvarks may run to escape predators. They can run up to twenty-five miles per hour.

Aardvark Cubs

Aardvarks usually have one baby, or cub. Cubs are born weighing about four pounds.

When they are first born, cubs drink milk from their mother. They are able to eat only insects by the time they are about three months old.

A cub stays with its mother for about six months. Then, it leaves to dig its own burrow.

Burrows

Aardvarks dig large burrows into the dirt. Their burrows have lots of tunnels and chambers.

When an aardvark goes out, it has a special **routine**. It looks out, then runs out and jumps up and down. Then, it runs back into the burrow and repeats the process. This helps it look for predators.

They stay in their burrows to stay out of the sun and safe from predators. They can also dig smaller burrows to quickly get away from predators.

Aardvark Life

Aardvarks are **solitary** animals.

They spend most of their time

alone.

They are also **nocturnal**. They

are most active at night and

are rarely seen during the day.

This helps them to stay out of

the hot sun and be safe from

predators.

Aardvarks may travel several miles each night looking for food.

Population

Aardvarks are not currently **endangered**, but their populations are **declining** in areas close to humans.

Their population is very important to their **ecosystem**. Many other animals depend on the burrows that aardvarks dig for shelter.

In the wild, aardvarks can live up to eighteen years. In **captivity,** they may live as long as twenty-three.

Aardvarks in Danger

Aardvarks face several threats from humans. The main threat is that their habitats are destroyed to make space for buildings and farmland.

They are also hunted for their meat. Some people believe that their teeth and bones can be used for magic or medicine.

Aardvarks that live close to humans often have a hard time finding enough food.

Helping Aardvarks

The African Wildlife Foundation is working to protect aardvark habitats. They are helping local people to find ways to live and farm without destroying habitats.

They also work to teach people about aardvarks. They want to stop the belief that they can be used for magic or medicine.

There are laws that help prevent aardvarks from being overhunted, but they don't stop all hunting of aardvarks.

It is important that aardvarks are kept safe from habitat loss and hunting. Their burrows are important for many other animals.

Glossary

Captivity: animals that are kept by humans, not in the wild

Declining: getting smaller

Ecosystem: a community of living things and the environment they live in

Endangered: at risk of becoming extinct

Insectivore: an animal that eats only insects

Larvae: insects that are not fully grown

Nocturnal: animals that are active and night

Predator: an animal that hunts other animals for food

Routine: a set of actions that are done regularly

Snout: the front part of an animals head that sticks out, includes the nose, mouth, and jaw

Solitary: living alone

About the Author

Victoria Blakemore is a first grade

teacher in Southwest Florida with a

passion for reading.

You can visit her at

www.elementaryexplorers.com

Also in This Series

Gray Wolves	Sloths	Flamingos	Camels	Koalas	Honey Bees	Pandas
Pangolins	White-Tailed Deer	Orcas	Giraffes	Corn	Meerkats	Echidnas
Walruses	Raccoons	Bald Eagles	Apples	Arctic Foxes	Red Pandas	Cassowaries
Tigers	Ladybugs	Moose	Beluga Whales	Leopards	Elephants	Jellyfish
Binturongs	Lions	Dolphins	Reindeer	Hammerhead Sharks	Hippos	Pumpkins
Peafowl	Chameleons	Florida Panthers	Aye-Ayes	Black Boars	Cheetahs	Manatees
Gingerbread	Polar Bears	Hot Chocolate	Orangutans	Coyotes	Marshmallows	Strawberries

Victoria Blakemore

Also in This Series

Aardvarks	Mako Sharks	Alligators	Frogs	Hedgehogs	Brown Bears	Bongos
Sea Turtles	Quokkas	Muskrats	Zebras	Red Foxes	Ring-Tailed Lemurs	Platypuses
Anteaters	Kangaroos	Rhinos	Jaguars	Wombats	Capybaras	Gorillas
Cats	Skunks	Butterflies	Dingoes	Snow Leopards	African Wild Dogs	Penguins
Whale Sharks	Wolverines	Warthogs	Caracals	Badgers	Seals	Hummingbirds
Pikas	Humpback Whales	Pumas	Lemonade	Llamas	Tulips	Ostriches
Sunflowers	Fennec Foxes	Sea Lions	Squirrels	Roses	Porcupines	Ice Cream

Elementary Explorers
Victoria Blakemore